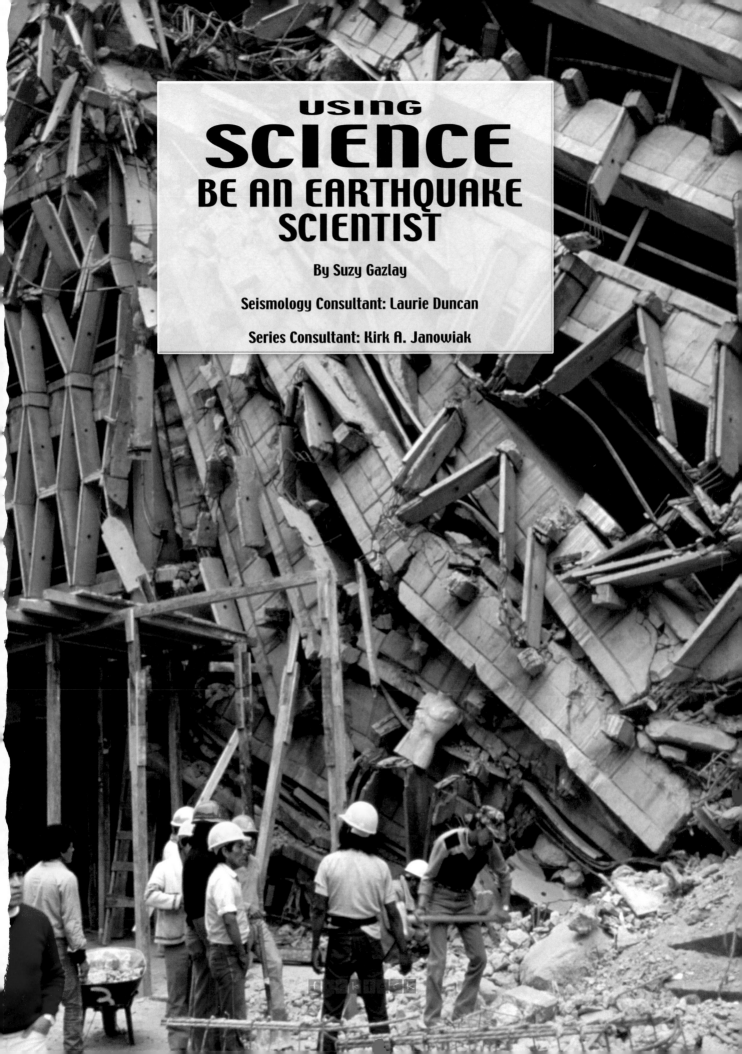

USING SCIENCE
BE AN EARTHQUAKE SCIENTIST

By Suzy Gazlay

Seismology Consultant: Laurie Duncan

Series Consultant: Kirk A. Janowiak

USING SCIENCE
BE AN EARTHQUAKE SCIENTIST

By: Suzy Gazlay

Consultant: Laurie Duncan

Series Consultant: Kirk A. Janowiak

ticktock project editor: Joe Harris

ticktock designer: James Powell

With thanks to: Sara Greasley

Copyright © ticktock Entertainment Ltd 2008

First published in Great Britain in 2008 by ticktock Media Ltd.,

Unit 2, Orchard Business Centre, North Farm Road, Tunbridge Wells, Kent, TN2 3XF

ISBN 978 1 84696 618 7 pbk
ISBN 978 1 84696 680 4 hbk

Printed in China

SUZY GAZLAY

Suzy Gazlay (MA Integrated Math/Science Education) is a teacher and writer who has worked with students of all ages. She has also served as a science specialist, curriculum developer, and consultant in varying capacities. She is the recipient of a Presidential Award for Excellence in Math and Science Teaching. Now retired from fulltime classroom teaching, she continues to write, consult, and work with educators and children, particularly in science and music education. Her many interests include music, environmental issues, marine biology, and the outdoors.

KIRK A. JANOWIAK

BS Biology & Natural Resources, MS Ecology & Animal Behavior, MS Science Education. Kirk has enjoyed teaching students from preschool through to college age. He has been awarded the National Association of Biology Teachers' Outstanding Biology Teacher Award and was honored to be a finalist for the Presidential Award for Math and Science Teaching. Kirk currently teaches Biology and Environmental Science and enjoys a wide range of interests from music to the art of roasting coffee.

LAURIE DUNCAN

Laurie Duncan (PhD Marine Geology and Geophysics) is a geology professor and science writer in Austin, Texas. Some of her research interests include seafloor mapping, active faults and earthquakes, plate tectonic boundaries, ocean currents and global sea level rise since the last ice age. In addition to teaching and writing about geology, nature and the outdoors, Laurie is interested in environmental policy issues. She is also an avid cyclist, rock climber and sometime mountaineer.

CONTENTS

This book supports the teaching of science at Key Stage 2 of the National Curriculum. Students will develop their understanding of these areas of scientific inquiry:

- Ideas and evidence in science
- Investigative skills
- Obtaining and presenting evidence
- Considering and evaluating evidence

Students will also learn about:

- Faults and fault zones
- Tectonic plates and plate movement
- The focus and epicentre of an earthquake
- Primary waves, secondary waves, and surface waves
- Seimographs and seismograms
- Finding the epicentre of a quake by triangulation
- The Modified Mercalli Intensity Scale
- Strike-slip and dip-slip movement
- Digging or drilling into a fault
- Protecting buildings from earthquakes
- Keeping safe during an earthquake
- How tsunamis are caused

HOW TO USE THIS BOOK

Science is important in the lives of people everywhere. We use science at home and at school – in fact, all the time. Everybody needs to know about science to understand how the world works. An earthquake scientist uses this understanding to predict the effects of earthquakes. They can also use science to protect us from events such as landslides and tsunamis. With this book you will use science to help officials prepare their city for a major earthquake.

This exciting science book is very easy to use – check out what's inside!

INTRODUCTION

Fun to read information about being an earthquake scientist.

FACTFILE

Easy to understand information about how and why earthquakes happen.

EARTHQUAKES ON THE OCEAN FLOOR

You've often explored and studied faults before and after quakes. It's one thing when the fault is on land, but what if it's on the ocean floor under hundreds of metres of water? You've been studying the fault beneath the city, but it's harder to look closely at the next section, which goes out to sea. Now you have the opportunity to go on a specially equipped research ship! You watch as an engineer prepares the ship's huge hollow drill.

FACTFILE

- The research ship is equipped with a drilling rig. This rises above the ship's deck like a tower.

- The ship's drill is lowered through hundreds of metres of seawater, to the ocean floor.

- The drill cuts around a long column of rock material called a core. This kind of drilling is like coring an apple.

- The core is transported up a pipe to the ship.

drill

sand   mud

20

4

WORKSTATION

Real-life earthquake science experiences, situations and problems for you to read about.

WORKSTATION

CORE SAMPLE

Approximate number of years ago

0
1,000
1,500
2,000
2,500
3,000
4,000
5,000
5,500
6,000

Wherever you can see mud under sand, there has been an earthquake.

This is ash from a volcanic eruption.

■ Mud   ■ Sand

You and other scientists are examining a 2.5-metre-long piece of core. It has been taken from a fault zone on the sea floor, 1.6 kilometres beneath the water level.

The sample shows how rock materials are layered on the ocean floor. It contains sediments dating back to 6,000 years ago. During that time, a pattern has been repeating over and over again.

The core taken from the ocean floor is brought on board the ship and prepared for study.

- The ocean floor is normally covered with mud.
- The mud is made of material that has settled on the bottom.
- A major earthquake occurs and triggers a landslide.
- Sand slides down and covers the mud.
- Over time, another layer of mud forms on top of the sand.

Q CHALLENGE QUESTIONS

1. How many major earthquakes are recorded in this core?
2. How long ago was the thickest layer of sand deposited?
3. How long ago was the thinnest sand layer put down? How do you think that quake might compare to the others?
4. How long ago did the volcano erupt?

21

IF YOU NEED HELP!

TIPS FOR SCIENCE SUCCESS

On page 30 you will find lots of tips to help you with your science work.

ANSWERS

Turn to page 31 to check your answers. (*Try all the activities and questions before you take a look at the answers.*)

GLOSSARY

On page 32 there is a glossary of earthquake science words.

Y ou are a seismologist – an earthquake scientist. A group of city officials has asked for your help. Several earthquakes have occurred in this city during the past 50 years. Two were strong enough to damage buildings. The officials are worried that an even worse earthquake – the Big One – may strike soon. They want to know if their city is likely to be struck by a major earthquake and, if so, when it might happen. They also ask your advice about how to make their city as safe as possible.

FACTFILE

- The Earth's outer surface is called the crust. It is broken into rigid sections called tectonic plates. They fit together like a jigsaw puzzle.

- A fault is where two blocks of rock move past each other.

- A fault zone is an area that contains many small faults. The fault zone may be thousands of metres wide. Earthquakes are likely to occur here.

- You know that the city is located in a fault zone.

This map shows the Earth's tectonic plates. Where they meet, there are fault zones.

This image shows the destruction caused by an earthquake in Mexico in 1985. This is the kind of damage that the Big One could cause to our city.

WORKSTATION

An earthquake is a sudden shaking of the ground. It occurs when two tectonic plates snap and slip past each other.

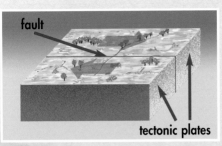

fault

tectonic plates

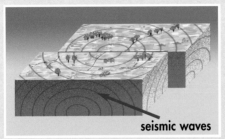

seismic waves

- When two tectonic plates try to slide past each other, friction stops them from moving smoothly.

- The plates suddenly jerk into a new position, and the pressure is released as seismic waves.

- The Earth's tectonic plates float on top of a flowing layer in Earth's mantle.

- Currents in the mantle cause the tectonic plates to slowly move. Sometimes they push together or pull apart. Sometimes they slide and scrape past each other.

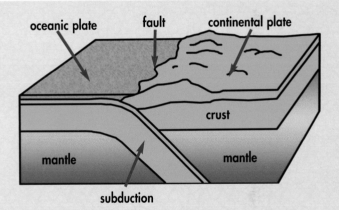

oceanic plate • fault • continental plate • crust • mantle • mantle • subduction

- The edge of one plate may go under the edge of another – this is called subduction.

- The strain of plate movement causes faults to form in the Earth's surface. If there is a major movement along a fault, we feel it as an earthquake.

Q CHALLENGE QUESTIONS

The city officials ask you some questions about earthquakes. Can you give them the right answers?

1. Why has the city suffered from earthquakes in the past?

2. What is a fault?

3. What happens when tectonic plates move into new positions?

4. What causes the tectonic plates to move?

EARTHQUAKES WORLDWIDE

If you are going to help the officials to protect their city, you will need access to the most accurate and up-to-date information about earthquakes. You decide to pay a visit to the National Geophysical Data Center (NGDC) in Boulder, Colorado. While you are there, a researcher shows you a map of the most powerful earthquakes since 1900.

The sudden movement of the plates creates vibrations that spread out in waves from a point deep underground that is called the focus. These waves produce the shaking and vibrations of an earthquake.

The area directly above the focus of the earthquake is the epicentre. This is where the strongest shaking occurs.

The fault: this is a break in the plate, where movement takes place.

The epicentre: this is the spot on the surface directly above the focus.

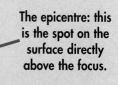

Seismic waves: these travel through the ground.

The focus: sharp movement here creates vibrations that spread out in waves.

This satellite image shows the San Andreas Fault in California.

WORKSTATION

There are 12 main tectonic plates plus about 40 smaller ones. The main ones are shown by the red lines on this map. The letters on the map show major earthquakes.

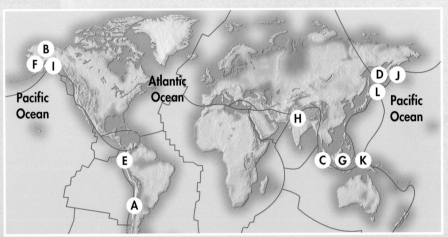

The strength and size of an earthquake are described by its magnitude. Magnitude is a measure of the total energy of an earthquake. This is calculated using the Moment Magnitude scale.

THE MOST POWERFUL EARTHQUAKES SINCE 1900			
	Location	Magnitude	Date
A	Chile, South America	9.5	22nd May, 1960
B	Alaska, USA	9.2	28th March, 1964
C	Indonesia, Asia	9.1	26th December, 2004
D	Kamchatka, Russia	9.0	4th November, 1952
E	Ecuador, South America	8.8	31st January, 1906
F	Alaska, USA	8.7	4th February, 1965
G	Indonesia, Asia	8.7	28th March, 2005
H	India-China border, Asia	8.6	15th August, 1950
I	Alaska, USA	8.6	9th March, 1957
J	Kamchatka, Russia	8.5	3rd February, 1923
K	Indonesia, Asia	8.5	1st February, 1938
L	Kuril Islands (Russia/Japan)	8.5	13th October, 1963

Q CHALLENGE QUESTIONS

1. Which was the strongest earthquake since 1900?

2. How many quakes measured 9.0 or more?

3. Where do the most earthquakes take place – around the Atlantic Ocean, or the Pacific Ocean?

4. Look at the positions of the earthquakes and tectonic plates. What do you notice about the way these earthquakes are grouped?

5. Where does the strongest shaking happen during an earthquake?

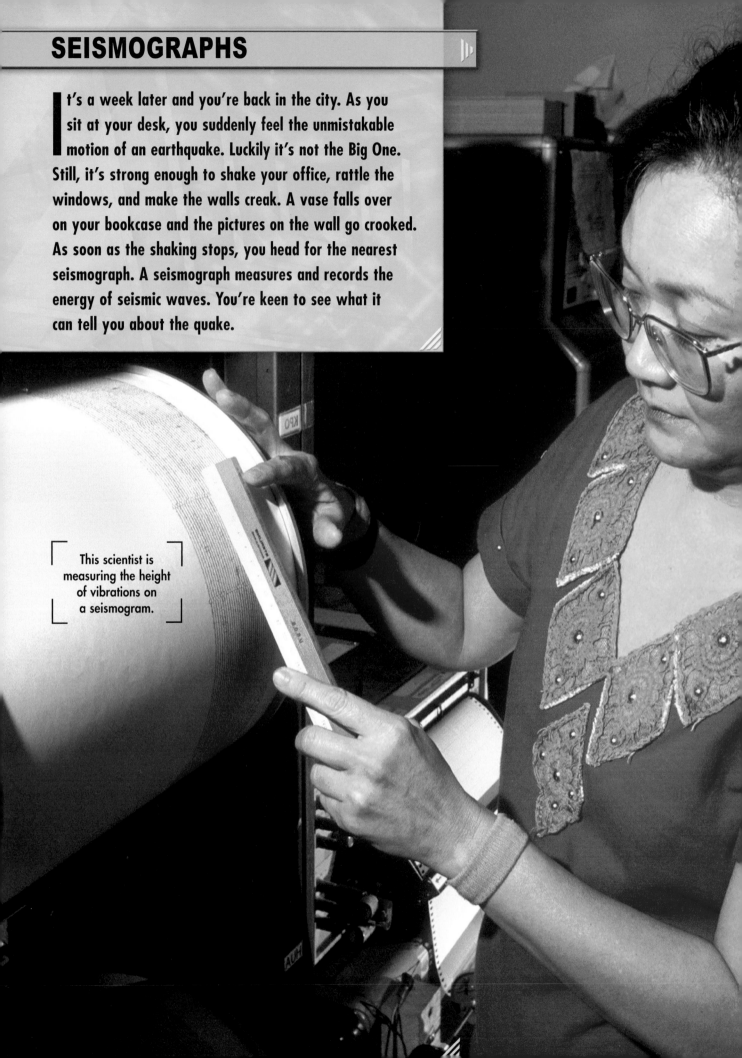

SEISMOGRAPHS

It's a week later and you're back in the city. As you sit at your desk, you suddenly feel the unmistakable motion of an earthquake. Luckily it's not the Big One. Still, it's strong enough to shake your office, rattle the windows, and make the walls creak. A vase falls over on your bookcase and the pictures on the wall go crooked. As soon as the shaking stops, you head for the nearest seismograph. A seismograph measures and records the energy of seismic waves. You're keen to see what it can tell you about the quake.

This scientist is measuring the height of vibrations on a seismogram.

WORKSTATION

Two types of seismic waves move inside the ground.

PRIMARY, OR P WAVES

SECONDARY, OR S WAVES

- These are the first waves that people feel. They travel fastest and arrive first. P waves push and pull the ground back and forth.

- P waves are followed by secondary, or S waves. S waves move the ground up and down, and from side to side.

- Surface waves travel on top of the ground. They move more slowly and arrive after P and S waves.

Here is the seismogram for the earthquake you just felt:

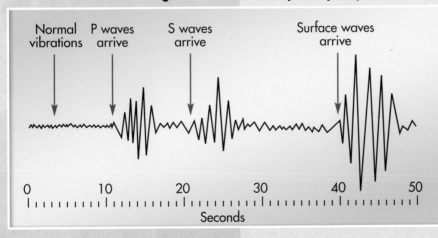

- The printed record from a seismograph is called a seismogram.
- The squiggles show vibrations. The more they move up and down, the stronger the quake.
- Different kinds of seismic waves travel at different speeds, and arrive at different times.

Q CHALLENGE QUESTIONS

You look closely at the seismogram.

1. Which kind of waves caused the strongest vibrations?

2. About how many seconds were there between the start of the P waves and the first S waves?

3. About how many seconds were there between the first P waves and the first surface waves?

11

FINDING THE EPICENTRE

You want to find the location of the epicentre of the earthquake. Was it within the city, or did the shaking you felt come from a break somewhere else along the fault? To find out where the epicentre was, you need two more seismograms of the same quake recorded at other locations nearby. You telephone some of your colleagues, who send you their readings. Now you can use the three seismograms to pinpoint the exact epicentre, using a technique called triangulation.

FACTFILE

The seismographs that you and your colleagues use look like the diagram below:

- When the ground shakes, the base and the drum move back and forth, but the hanging weight stays still.

- As the base moves, the pen writes on the drum.

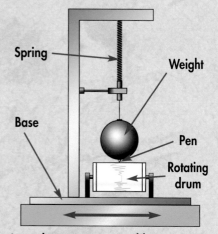

Horizontal movement caused by seismic waves

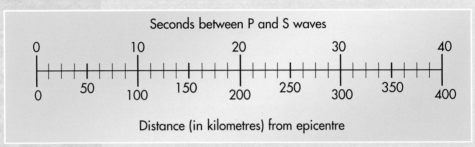
> Sometimes the movement of earthquakes causes cracks to appear in the ground.

CHALLENGE A: DISTANCE

You want to find out where the epicentre of the earthquake was.
First you need to find out how far the epicentre was from your seismograph.

This scale shows that the further you are from an epicentre, the longer the time will be between the P and S waves.

Seconds between P and S waves

0　　　　10　　　　20　　　　30　　　　40

0　　50　　100　150　200　250　300　350　400

Distance (in kilometres) from epicentre

1. Look back at your answer to question 2 on page 11. How many seconds were there between the start of the P waves and the start of the S waves on your seismogram? Now find that number of seconds on the scale. Approximately how far was your seismograph from the epicentre?

2. You are at Alpha Town. On the seismogram from Betaville, there are 30 seconds between the start of the P Waves and the start of the S Waves. The seismogram from Gamma City measures 20 seconds between them. Approximately how far are Betaville and Gamma City from the epicentre?

CHALLENGE B: TRIANGULATION

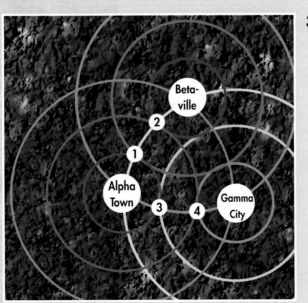

3. This map shows the locations of Alpha Town, Betaville and Gamma City. The rings around each city show distances of 100, 200 and 300 kilometres. Can you figure out which ring shows the distance to the epicentre from each city?

Now can you find a place where those three rings meet? Write down the number marking that place. That is the epicentre of the earthquake!

EYEWITNESS DATA: INTENSITY

During the next few days, you talk to many people. Some were near the epicentre of the quake and some were as far away as several hundred kilometres. You ask them where they were when the quake hit and what they experienced. You get quite a range of answers!

A "Bottles and cans came crashing off the high shelves. The big front window cracked."

Alice, shopper, in market

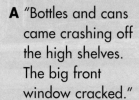

B "The windows creaked and the room shook a little. The teacher told us to get under our desks."

Ben, student, in classroom

C "Everyone ran outside. The old brick building next door was pretty badly damaged."

Chantrelle, accountant, in office

D "I felt it, but it wasn't very strong. I thought it was a big truck going by."

Dan, trainer, in gym

E "Some people ran outside. The only damage I saw was a chimney that fell down."

Eddie, police officer, on street

F "I didn't feel a thing. I didn't even know about it until I heard about it later."

Frederico, mechanic, in garage

An earthquake can be measured by its **magnitude**, which describes how much energy it releases. It can also be described by its **intensity** – the strength of shaking at a certain location.

- The intensity of a quake gets weaker the further you are from the epicentre. The magnitude of a quake is the same no matter where you are.
- Intensity is measured by the Modified Mercalli Intensity scale.

MODIFIED MERCALLI INTENSITY SCALE		Magnitude Scale
I	Detected only by sensitive instruments.	1.5
II	Vibrations are felt by some people at rest, especially on upper floors. Hanging objects may swing.	2
III	Vibrations felt noticeably indoors, but not always recognised as earthquake. Stationary cars rock slightly. The vibrations feel similar to a passing lorry.	2.5
IV	Many people indoors feel the vibrations, but few outdoors. At night some people may wake up. Dishes, windows and doors move. Cars rock noticeably.	3
V	Felt by most people. Dishes, windows and plaster may break. Tall objects sway.	3.5
VI	Felt by everyone. Many people are frightened and run outdoors. There is falling plaster and chimneys, but damage is small.	4
VII	Everybody runs outdoors. Damage to buildings varies depending on quality of construction. The vibrations are felt by people driving cars.	4.5
VIII	Walls, monuments and chimneys may fall. Drivers have difficulty controlling cars.	5
IX	Cracks appear in buildings, and they are shifted off their foundations. The ground cracks and underground pipes are broken.	5.5
X	Most brick and wooden buildings are destroyed. Rails bend, and landslides happen.	6
XI	Few buildings remain standing. Bridges are destroyed, and cracks open in the ground. Pipes are broken.	6.5
XII	Total devastation. Waves are seen travelling across the ground. Objects are thrown up into air.	7
		7.5
		8

Q CHALLENGE QUESTION

You have interviewed a lot of people about their experiences. Six of them are shown to the left. Can you give each of these people a Mercalli number?

LOOKING AT FAULT MOVEMENT

A s a seismologist, you have developed keen observation skills. You want to see more than a paper map of a fault. You can walk along a fault zone and, like a detective, gather clues that show how the ground has moved along the fault. Sometimes the clues you spot are hundreds or even thousands of years old. Sometimes, especially soon after a strong quake, the signs can be very dramatic.

FACTFILE

- Where you find a fissure – a crack in the ground – you measure it to see whether it has become wider.

- You also look for such things as a bank of earth where a section of ground has dropped, or a fence that no longer connects in a straight line.

- Even certain types of cracks in the pavement can be important clues.

There are two basic types of movement along a fault.

- One type of fault movement is sideways, or strike-slip movement. The movement can be either to the right or to the left.

STRIKE-SLIP MOVEMENT

- Movement along a fault can also go up or down. This is known as dip-slip movement. If one side of the fault drops down, it's called a normal fault. If one side is pushed up over the other side, it's called a reverse fault. Either way, one side of the fault ends up higher than the other.

DIP-SLIP MOVEMENT

NORMAL FAULT

DIP-SLIP MOVEMENT

REVERSE FAULT

Q CHALLENGE QUESTIONS

Can you tell what kind of fault movement has occurred in each of these pictures? Which ones show strike-slip movement? Which ones show dip-slip movement?

1

2

3

4

DIGGING INTO THE FAULT

What better way to get first-hand information about a fault than to go down inside it? You join some other scientists, who are studying a trench that has been dug right across the fault. Down inside, you can take a close look at this fault and the smaller ones that connect to it. You'll want to measure and identify the different types of rock you see. Most of all, you want to find out about past movement along this section of the fault.

FACTFILE

- Digging into a trench is like digging into history – the deeper you dig, the further you travel into the past.

- You can use information about past quakes to predict when the next quake might hit, where, and how big it might be.

800

WORKSTATION

You watch as a backhoe digs the trench.

- Then you and your coworkers can climb down, and take measurements, samples, and pictures.
- You discover that the most recent major earthquake happened 780 years ago.

Sand	Coarse gravel
Silt	Sandy gravel
— Fault	

This section of the trench wall is six feet wide and ten feet tall.

You can see when earthquakes took place by looking at different layers of rock in the trench wall.

- New soil and rock is added to the surface of the ground at a steady rate. Over time, various different kinds of rock have settled – these are represented in the diagram by different colours.
- You can tell that an earthquake happened when you find a sudden change in the level of the rock.
- Look at the coarse gravel layer. When this was on the surface, an earthquake happened. One side of the fault moved up, and the other moved down.
- To figure out how long ago an earthquake happened, you must measure how much soil and rock have piled up on top of the layer where the earthquake took place.

Q CHALLENGE QUESTIONS

This photograph shows the same section of the trench as the diagram above.
Can you match each statement to a letter on the diagram?

1. An earthquake occurred in this layer.
2. This is the most recent layer.
3. This layer is made up of sand.
4. This is the line of the fault.

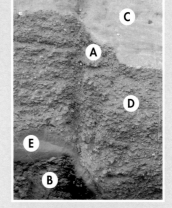

1857

1812

1100

This scientist is pointing to a spot where you can see an earthquake has occurred.

The labels on the wall of the trench show the dates of past earthquakes.

EARTHQUAKES ON THE OCEAN FLOOR

You've often explored and studied faults before and after quakes. It's one thing when the fault is on land, but what if it's on the ocean floor under hundreds of metres of water? You've been studying the fault beneath the city, but it's harder to look closely at the next section, which goes out to sea. Now you have the opportunity to go on a specially equipped research ship! You watch as an engineer prepares the ship's huge hollow drill.

 FACTFILE

- The research ship is equipped with a drilling rig. This rises above the ship's deck like a tower.
- The ship's drill is lowered through hundreds of metres of seawater, to the ocean floor.
- The drill cuts around a long column of rock material called a core. This kind of drilling is like coring an apple.
- The core is transported up a pipe to the ship.

drill

sand   mud

CORE SAMPLE

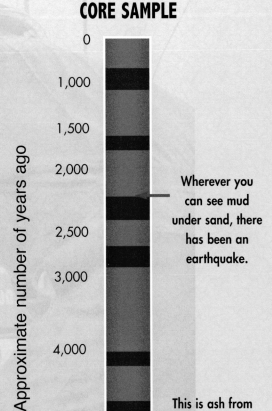

Approximate number of years ago

0
1,000
1,500
2,000
2,500
3,000
4,000
5,000
5,500
6,000

Wherever you can see mud under sand, there has been an earthquake.

 This is ash from a volcanic eruption.

 Mud   Sand

You and other scientists are examining a 2.5-metre-long piece of core. It has been taken from a fault zone on the sea floor, 1.6 kilometres beneath the water level.

The sample shows how rock materials are layered on the ocean floor. It contains sediments dating back to 6,000 years ago. During that time, a pattern has been repeating over and over again.

The core taken from the ocean floor is brought on board the ship and prepared for study.

- The ocean floor is normally covered with mud.
- The mud is made of material that has settled on the bottom.
- A major earthquake occurs and triggers a landslide.
- Sand slides down and covers the mud.
- Over time, another layer of mud forms on top of the sand.

Q CHALLENGE QUESTIONS

1. How many major earthquakes are recorded in this core?
2. How long ago was the thickest layer of sand deposited?
3. How long ago was the thinnest sand layer put down? How do you think that quake might compare to the others?
4. How long ago did the volcano erupt?

PREPARING FOR THE BIG ONE

You visit the city officials to share with them what you have discovered from your research. You tell them what you have learned about the fault beneath their city. You also tell them that a serious quake, even the Big One, could happen very soon. They will have to do everything they can to prepare the city for this possibility!

If buildings are built on the wrong sort of ground, their columns may sink during an earthquake.
This parking garage was destroyed by a major earthquake in California, in 1994.

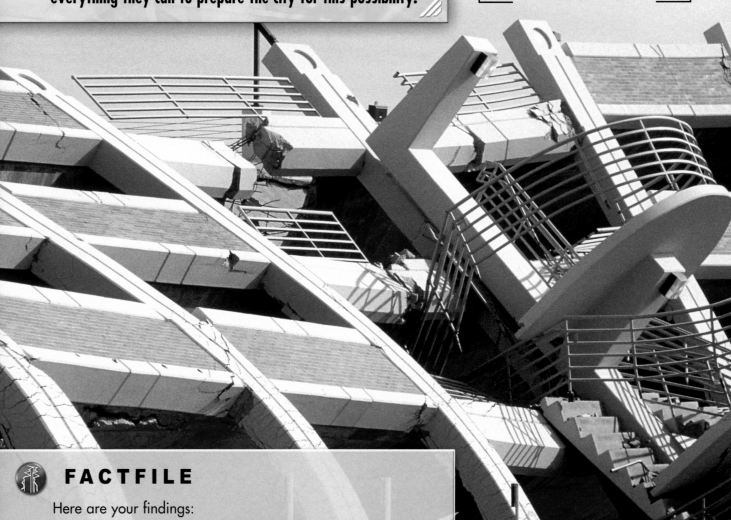

FACTFILE

Here are your findings:

- From your seismogram reading, you know that the city was only 100 kilometres from the epicentre of a recent quake. It is likely to be seriously damaged in the event of a larger earthquake.

- You examined a core sample from the ocean floor. This told you that there have been 8 major earthquakes in the last 6,000 years. This means that a major earthquake has happened about every 750 years.

- By digging into the fault, you discovered that the last major earthquake happened 780 years ago. This means that the city is overdue for another major quake – the Big One.

You have made a list of observations from studying quake damage to buildings. You use this to give the officials some advice.

- Most of the damage during a quake is caused by the ground shaking. But not all ground is alike, even in the same part of a city. Some kinds of earth material will shake more than others.

- Structures built on hard bedrock such as granite shake the least and are most likely to survive.

- Deep, loose soil shakes more than bedrock.

- The most heavily damaged buildings are usually built on wet, sandy soil or landfill.

You show the officials a map of their city.

The different colours show the intensity of shaking that might be expected during a major quake with a magnitude of 7.5. The amount of shaking will vary according to the type of earth material in each area.

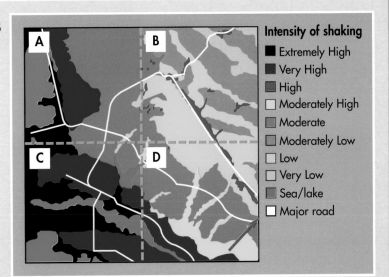

Intensity of shaking
- Extremely High
- Very High
- High
- Moderately High
- Moderate
- Moderately Low
- Low
- Very Low
- Sea/lake
- Major road

Q CHALLENGE QUESTIONS

The city needs to build a new hospital. The city officials ask you where would be the best place to put it.

1. Look at the map above. Which part of the city (A, B, C or D) would be the best place to build the new hospital?

2. Which part of the city would be a particularly dangerous place to build the hospital?

3. Which is the best kind of ground to build on?

4. Which kind of ground is the most dangerous to build on?

THE BIG ONE STRIKES!

A year later, you return to the city to check on their preparations for the Big One. You wake in the middle of the night to find your bed is moving across the floor. You hear a low rumbling which gets louder and louder. All around your hotel room, objects are crashing to the floor. The windows rattle and then shatter. The Big One has hit, and you are right in the middle of it! You scramble out of bed and crawl under the heavy desk in the corner. You can only hope that the building does not come down with you in it.

The earthquake causes destruction throughout the city. Later you discover that the building opposite your hotel was shaken off its foundations, and crushed a car.

You know that it's important to stay calm during an earthquake. Sometimes you visit schools to talk about earthquake safety, and this is the advice that you give the students.

- If you are inside, duck, cover, and hold. Duck down on the floor. Take cover under a sturdy table or desk. Hold on to it in case you need to move with it. Stay away from glass, windows, and anything that might fall or break. Don't move until the shaking stops.

- If you are outside, move into an open area away from buildings and power lines. Falling power lines could electrocute you.

- If you are in a car, ask the driver to stop where it is safe, out of the traffic. Stay away from bridges, tunnels, and overpasses. Don't stop under power lines, trees, or street lamps.

- If you are in the mountains or near any cliffs, watch out for landslides and falling rocks.

Q CHALLENGE QUESTIONS

An earthquake has struck. What are the potential dangers in each picture? What might happen?

1
2
3
4
5

25

TSUNAMI

The hotel you are staying in is on the seafront. When the shaking stops you look out of the broken window at the ocean. You know that when there is a strong quake (magnitude 7.5 or higher) near or beneath the ocean, there is the possibility of a tsunami. The water has gone out a long way, further than at low tide – this is a sure sign that a tsunami is on its way!

The artist's impression shows what it would be like to witness a major tsunami. Luckily the tsunami that hits your city is not this serious!

 FACTFILE

- Tsunamis are created when an earthquake shakes the seabed, which sets a huge amount of water into motion.

- Waves spread out in all directions, travelling as fast as 800 kilometres per hour.

- The waves out in the open ocean are often less than a metre tall. As the water gets shallower the waves get higher. When they reach land, they can reach as high as 30 metres tall!

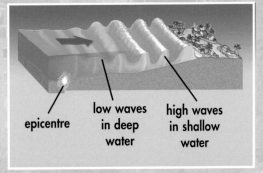

epicentre   low waves in deep water   high waves in shallow water

WORKSTATION

As you watch, a high wave crashes against the shore. But the damage is nowhere near as bad as you feared. There is some flooding, but the buildings along the seafront are protected by barriers.

An average of about 10 tsunamis form every year, worldwide, but most of these run out of energy before they ever reach shore. The intensity of a tsunami is measured by its wave height just before it reaches the shore.

Wave height	Effect	Frequency
0.5 metres	Not noticed.	Often happens.
1 metre	Low-lying coastal areas may be flooded.	Happens every four to eight months.
4 metres	Flooding, damage to buildings. Lots of debris and litter.	Happens about once a year.
8 metres	Small buildings are destroyed, and large ones are damaged. Fish are washed ashore. Some people may drown.	About once every three years.
15 metres	Nearly all buildings totally destroyed. Trees are uprooted. Many people drown.	About once every ten years.

This graph shows the number of tsunamis worldwide, from 1950 to 1999.

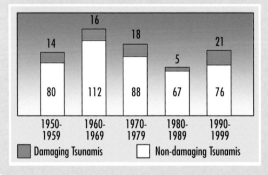

	1950-1959	1960-1969	1970-1979	1980-1989	1990-1999
Damaging Tsunamis	14	16	18	5	21
Non-damaging Tsunamis	80	112	88	67	76

Q CHALLENGE QUESTIONS

1. How are the waves in a tsunami created?

2. How high would a tsunami wave have to be to destroy small buildings?

3. Which ten-year period had the most total tsunamis? Which had the least?

4. Which ten-year period had the most damaging tsunamis? The least?

AFTER THE QUAKE

When you are sure it is safe, you venture outside. Everywhere you look, there is chaos – broken power lines, cars crushed under debris, and collapsed buildings. With a group of other scientists, you set out to assess the earthquake damage. There have been some casualties, but many lives have been saved by your advice. You're pleased to hear that the new hospital was undamaged by the quake.

FACTFILE

- The quake had a magnitude of 7.4.
- More than a million earthquakes happen each year, but most of them are too minor to be noticed.
- About 18 major earthquakes, with a magnitude of 7 or more, happen each year.

Your work isn't done quite yet. You inspect every building with damage to find out what went wrong.

You take a photo of each to put with your description of the damage. Sooner or later, there will be another quake. What you learn from this one will help the city do even better next time.

Q CHALLENGE QUESTIONS

Can you match each of these descriptions to one of the photos above? How might this kind of damage be prevented in future?

1. The supports of this bridge were built on soft muddy ground.

2. The walls on the bottom level of this new house were weak.

3. The supports on this bridge were solid, but the design of bridge did not stand up to shaking.

4. The front wall of this building was not reinforced and has collapsed from the shaking.

TIPS FOR SCIENCE SUCCESS

Pages 8-9

Earthquakes Worldwide

The National Geophysical Data Center (NGDC) deals with all sorts of information related to studying our planet. They study earthquakes, volcanoes, lakes, oceans, tsunamis, the climate, and natural disasters.

Pages 10-11

Seismographs

Seismograph technology has come a long way! The very first seismograph was a 'dragon jar' invented in China around 132 AD. Eight dragonheads were arranged around the brim of the jar. Each had a ball in its mouth. Directly beneath each dragonhead was an open-mouthed frog. When an earthquake took place, the shaking caused a ball to drop from a dragon's mouth into the mouth of the frog.

Pages 14-15

Eyewitness Data: Intensity

The Modified Mercalli Intensity scale uses Roman numerals. This is a counting system which was used in ancient Rome. It is easy to read once you know how. I = 1, V = 5, and X = 10. If a smaller number comes before a larger one, you subtract the smaller one from the larger one: IX = 9. Otherwise you just add them up: VI = 6.
The Roman numerals on the Mercalli scale are: I (1), II (2), III (3), IV (4), V (5), VI (6), VII (7), VIII (8), IX (9), X (10), XI (11), and XII (12).

Pages 16-17

Looking at Fault Movement

Think about a road running straight across a fault line. An earthquake takes place.

- If the fault movement is strike-slip, the road on one side of the fault will move to the left and the other side will move to the right.
- If the fault movement is dip-slip, there will be a break across the road. The road on one side of the break will be higher than the road on the other side.

Pages 18-19

Digging into the Fault

Layers of rocks in an area that hasn't had earthquakes or other disturbances over the years will look like bands of different coloured rock material running sideways. If there has been an earthquake, you'll be able to see where the layers in place at the time were broken and displaced. Over the years after the earthquake, more rock material will be deposited on top of the old layers, gradually levelling out the surface of the ground again.

Pages 20-21

Earthquakes on the Ocean Floor

The core sample shown is just one section of an entire core. You can see from the photo that an entire core is quite long – nearly 10 metres! The inside of the drillpipe is lined with plastic. When the core is taken out of the pipe, the plastic wrap keeps it all together like a very long sandwich.

Pages 28-29

After the Quake

With a magnitude of 7.4, this is a big quake, but a bigger quake may still come. A quake like this one is likely to have relieved some pressure along the fault, but more pressure will continue to build. The officials will always need to keep earthquakes in mind as they make decisions about the city.

Pages 6-7
1. The city has suffered from earthquakes because it is located in a fault zone.
2. A place where two blocks of rock move past each other.
3. The pressure is released as seismic waves, causing an earthquake.
4. Currents in the mantle.

Pages 8-9
1. The earthquake in Chile on 22nd May, 1960.
2. Four.
3. More earthquakes happen around the rim of the Pacific Ocean. This area is sometimes called the 'Ring of Fire'.
4. The strongest earthquakes have taken place near the edges of tectonic plates.
5. At the epicentre.

Pages 10-11
1. The surface waves.
2. 10 seconds.
3. 29 seconds.

Pages 12-13
1. 100 kilometres.
2. Betaville is 300 kilometres from the earthquake; Gamma City is 200 kilometres away.
3. The epicentre is at point 3.

Pages 14-15
A. Alice – V.
B. Ben – IV.
C. Chantrelle – VII.
D. Dan – III.
E. Eddie – VI.
F. Frederico – I.

Pages 16-17
1. Strike-slip movement.
2. Dip-slip movement.
3. Dip-slip movement.
4. Strike-slip movement.

Pages 18-19
1. B – the coarse gravel layer.
2. C – the silt layer. You can tell it is the most recent layer because it is at the top.
3. E.
4. A.

Pages 20-21
1. 8 major earthquakes.
2. 3,000 years ago.
3. 2,500 years ago. Less sand was deposited, because this earthquake was not as strong as the others and created less of a landslide.
4. 5,000 years ago.

Pages 22-23
1. Area B would be the safest place to build the hospital.
2. The most dangerous areas of the map for building would be area C.
3. Hard bedrock like granite.
4. Sandy soil or landfill.

Pages 24-25
1. There is a risk of landslides in the mountains and near cliffs.
2. Keep away from bridges, which might collapse.
3. You should steer clear of power lines during an earthquake, since they could fall down and electrocute you.
4. Windows may smash during an earthquake – you could be hurt by the broken glass.
5. There is a danger that trees might fall on you during an earthquake.

Pages 26-27
1. When the seabed is hit by an earthquake, a huge amount of water is set in motion, creating waves. As the waves move into shallower water, they get higher.
2. 8 metres high.
3. 1960-1969 had the most tsunamis. 1980-89 had the fewest.
4. 1990-1999 had the most damaging tsunamis. 1980-1989 had the fewest.

Pages 28-29
1. B. In future, make sure that bridge supports are built on firm ground.
2. A. The walls of houses must be made of a strong enough material.
3. C. Bridges must be designed to withstand shaking.
4. D. The outer walls of houses must be reinforced.

BEDROCK Solid rock underneath the surface of the ground.

CRUST The outer layer of rock that makes up the surface of the Earth.

CURRENT The flow of a substance in one specific direction.

EPICENTRE A point on the Earth's surface that is directly above the focus, the underground spot where the earthquake begins.

FAULT A break in the Earth's crust, where two blocks of rock move past each other.

FAULT ZONE An area where many faults are connected together, usually along the boundary between tectonic plates.

FOCUS The point beneath the Earth's surface where an earthquake begins.

FRICTION The force that keeps objects from moving past each other.

INTENSITY The strength of an earthquake as it is felt at the surface.

MAGNITUDE A measurement of energy released during an earthquake.

MANTLE The thick layer of rock beneath the Earth's crust.

MODIFIED MERCALLI INTENSITY SCALE A scale of earthquake intensity based on what people feel or observe during a quake.

MOMENT MAGNITUDE SCALE A scale used by scientists to compare the magnitude of earthquakes.

PRESSURE A physical force put on or against an object, from something touching it.

SEDIMENTS Loose particles of rock.

SEISMIC WAVES Vibrations that travel through the Earth.

SEISMOGRAM The printed record of the information recorded by a seismograph.

SEISMOGRAPH An instrument that measures and records vibrations in the Earth at a specific location.

SEISMOLOGIST A geologist (earth scientist) who specialises in the study of earthquakes, seismic waves, and the effects of earthquakes.

TECTONIC PLATES A series of rigid plates that make up Earth's outer shell.

TSUNAMI A series of large waves caused by an earthquake, volcanic eruption, or landslide beneath or near the ocean.

PICTURE CREDITS

Picture credits (a=above; b=below or bottom; c=centre; f=far; l=left; r=right; t=top)

Corbis 16-17 (main), 18-19 (main). Getty 8-9 (main), 25tr. IODP/TAMU 20-21 (main), 20bc, 21cr. National Oceanic and Atmospheric Administration/Department of Commerce 17bcl, 17bcr, 17bl, 17br, 27cl. Rex features 6-7 (main), 28-29 (main). Royal Observatory of Belgium 19br. Science Photo Library 1 (main), 10-11 (main) 12-13 (main) 22-23 (main) 24-25 (main). Shutterstock 14-15 (main), 14tc, 14tr, 14cl, 14c, 14bl, 14br, 25bfl, 25bl, 25bc, 25br, 25bfr, 26-27 (main), 30-31 (main). Ticktock Media Archive 6bl, 7tr, 7cr, 7tl, 8bl, 9tr, 10bl, 11tr, 11tl, 11cl, 12bl, 13bl, 17tr, 17acr, 17acl, 19cl, 20b, 21cl, 23c, 26bl, 31bl. USGS 2t, 19t, 23acr, 23tr, 29acl, 29acr, 29bcl, 29bcr, 30cl.

Every effort has been made to trace the copyright holders, and we apologize in advance for any unintentional omissions. We would be pleased to insert the appropriate acknowledgments in any subsequent edition of this publication.